Navigating the Bulls and Bears:

A Guide to Stock Market Success
(Vol. – 1)

Acknowledgements

Writing ***"Navigating the Bulls and Bears: A Guide to Stock Market Success"*** has been an inspiring and fulfilling journey. We would like to express our deepest gratitude to everyone who contributed to the creation of this book.

First and foremost, we want to thank our readers for investing their time and interest in learning about the stock market. Your enthusiasm for understanding the complexities of investing has been the driving force behind this project.

We extend our heartfelt appreciation to the team at our publisher for their unwavering support, guidance, and belief in the value of this book. Their expertise and dedication have been instrumental in shaping this comprehensive guide.

We are deeply grateful to the financial experts and investment professionals who generously shared their insights and knowledge, contributing to the richness and accuracy of the content. Your expertise has added immeasurable value to this book.

Special thanks go to our families and friends for their patience, encouragement, and unwavering support throughout this writing process. Your belief in our abilities kept us motivated during challenging times.

Lastly, we want to acknowledge the tireless efforts of our editorial and research teams who diligently worked to ensure the accuracy and coherence of the content. Your attention to detail and commitment to excellence have made this book possible.

We dedicate this book to all the aspiring investors who seek to navigate the stock market with confidence and prudence. May "Navigating the Bulls and Bears: A Guide to Stock Market Success" empower you to make informed decisions, achieve your financial aspirations, and embark on a successful investment journey.

Thank you to all who have been part of this endeavor. Your support and contributions have enriched this book, and we are truly grateful for your involvement.

Sincerely,

Ritesh Bahry

Contents

CHAPTER 1:
Understanding the Bulls and Bears:
An Introduction to Market Cycles

Introduction:

Welcome to the exciting world of the stock market! As a beginner investor, it's essential to grasp the concept of market cycles and how they impact the prices of stocks. In this chapter, we will delve into the two dominant forces in the stock market: bulls and bears. Understanding these market cycles will lay the groundwork for your successful journey in navigating the stock market.

1.1 What are Bulls and Bears?

In the stock market, bulls and bears are commonly used terms to describe the prevailing market sentiments. A bull market refers to a period when the market is on an upward trend, characterized by rising asset prices and positive investor confidence. During a bull market, investors believe that the market will continue to grow and, therefore, show a strong interest in buying stocks and other assets.

On the other hand, a bear market is a period of decline in the market, characterized by falling asset prices and a general sense of pessimism among investors. In a bear market, investors expect further declines and are more inclined to sell their holdings to protect their capital.

Understanding these terms is crucial because they form the basis for analyzing market trends and determining appropriate investment strategies.

1.2 Characteristics of Bull Markets:

In this section, we will explore the key characteristics of bull markets:

a. Economic Growth: Bull markets are often associated with periods of robust economic growth. Companies tend to report increasing revenues and profits, driving stock prices higher.

b. Positive Investor Sentiment: During a bull market, investors feel optimistic about the future of the economy and the companies they invest in. This positive sentiment encourages more people to enter the market and buy stocks.

c. Rising Stock Prices: Bull markets are marked by a sustained uptrend in stock prices, creating wealth for investors and attracting more capital into the market.

d. Low Unemployment: Bull markets are often accompanied by low unemployment rates, indicating a healthy job market and increased consumer spending.

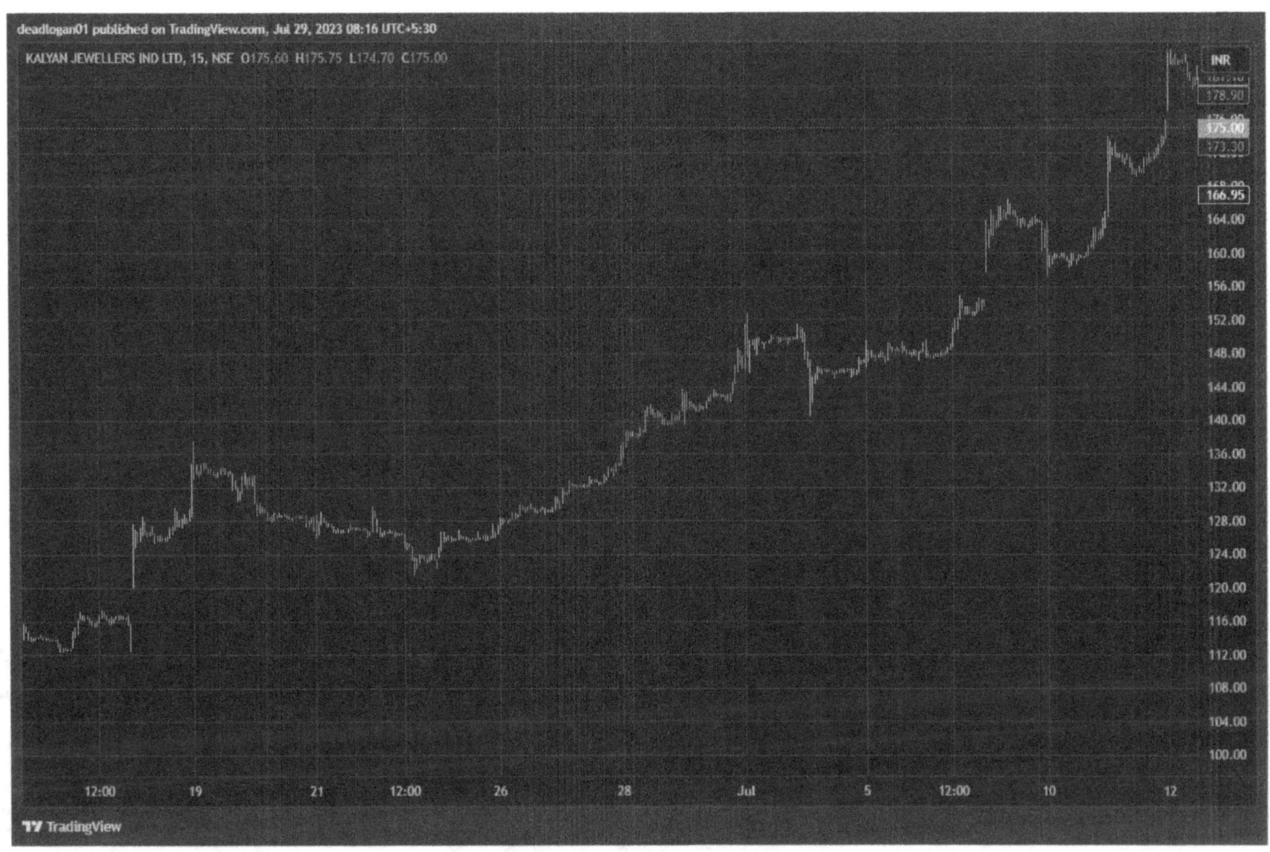

Image 1.2.1: Chart of KALYAN JEWELLERS IND Ltd showing a Bull Run.

1.3 Characteristics of Bear Markets:

Now, let's examine the main characteristics of bear markets:

a. Economic Contractions: Bear markets are typically associated with economic downturns or recessions. Companies may experience declining revenues and profits, leading to a decrease in stock prices.

b. Negative Investor Sentiment: During a bear market, fear and uncertainty grip the investors. Many become cautious and may choose to sell their stocks, further contributing to the market decline.

c. Falling Stock Prices: In a bear market, stock prices tend to decline over an extended period, eroding investor wealth and making it challenging to find profitable investment opportunities.

d. High Unemployment: Bear markets are often accompanied by rising unemployment rates, as companies may cut costs and reduce their workforce during economic slowdowns.

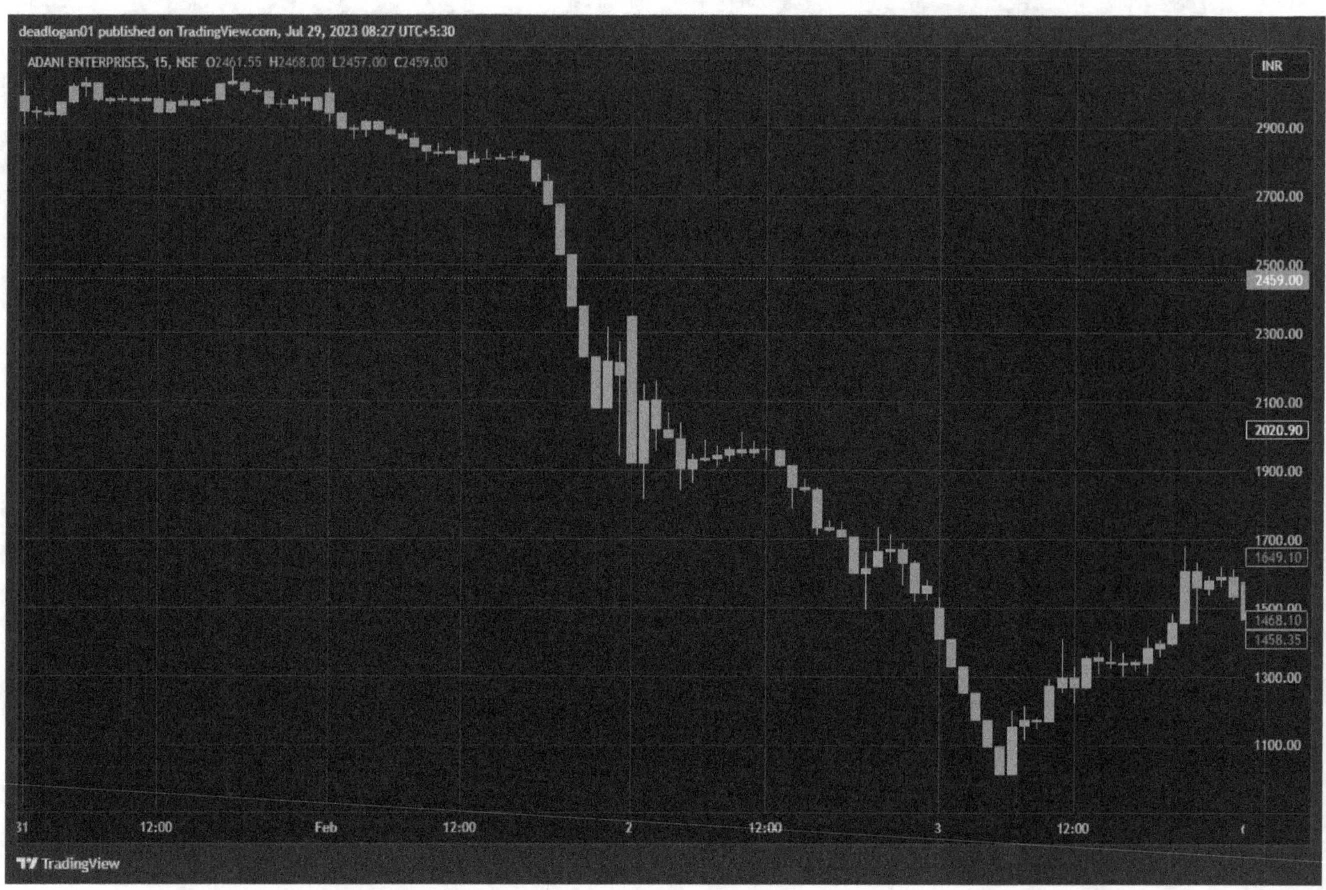

Image 1.2.2: Chart of ADANI ENERPRISES showing a Bear Run.

1.4 Transitioning Between Bulls and Bears:

Market cycles are not static, and transitions between bull and bear markets can happen due to various factors. Some common triggers for these transitions include :

a. Economic Indicators: Key economic indicators, such as GDP growth, inflation rates, and consumer confidence, can influence market cycles.

b. Geopolitical Events: Political instability, trade tensions, or global events can have significant effects on market sentiment.

c. Central Bank Policies: Actions taken by central banks, such as interest rate changes or monetary policy adjustments, can impact investor behavior and market cycles.

Understanding the factors that drive transitions between bulls and bears is essential for anticipating market movements and making informed investment decisions.

1.5 Historical Examples:

To gain a broader perspective, let's examine historical examples of bull and bear markets:

a. The Roaring Twenties (Bull Market): The 1920s saw a period of remarkable economic growth and soaring stock prices. However, it ended with the devastating crash of 1929, leading to the Great Depression.

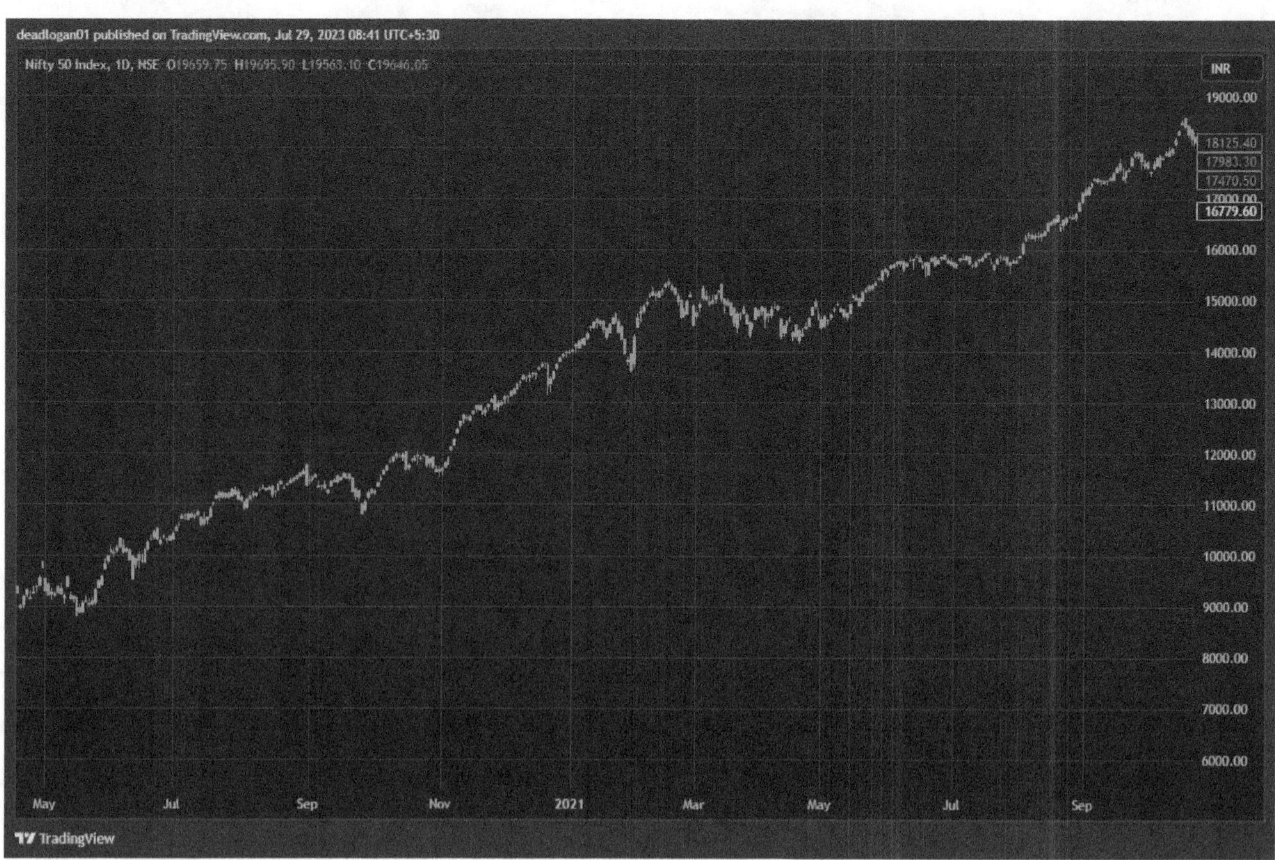

Image 1.5.1: Chart of NIFTY 50 showing the Bull Run of *"The Roaring Twenties"*

b. The Dotcom Bubble (Bear Market): In the late 1990s, there was a speculative frenzy in internet-based companies, leading to overinflated stock prices. The bubble burst in the early 2000s, resulting in a bear market.

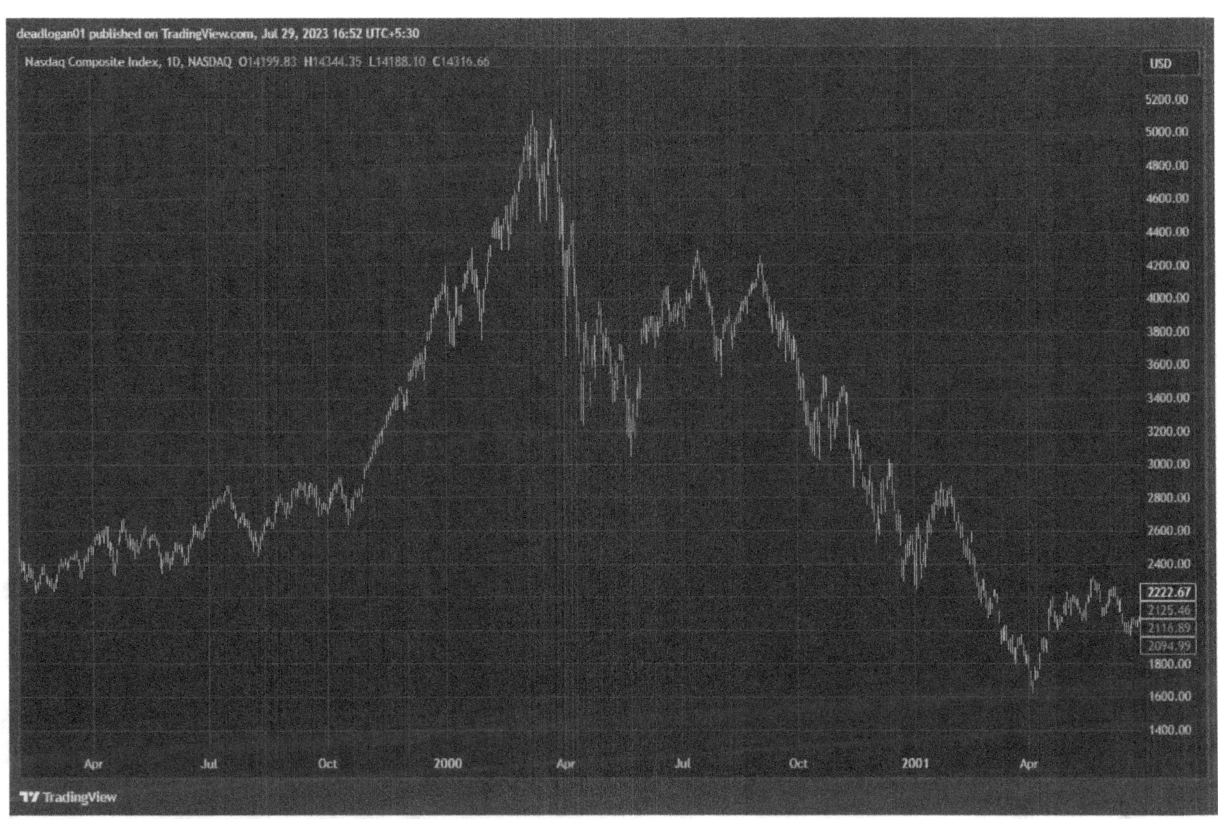

Image 1.5.2: Chart of NASDAQ showing *"The Dotcom Bubble"* in US

c. The Global Financial Crisis (Bear Market): The 2008 financial crisis was triggered by the collapse of the housing market and led to a severe bear market, impacting economies worldwide.

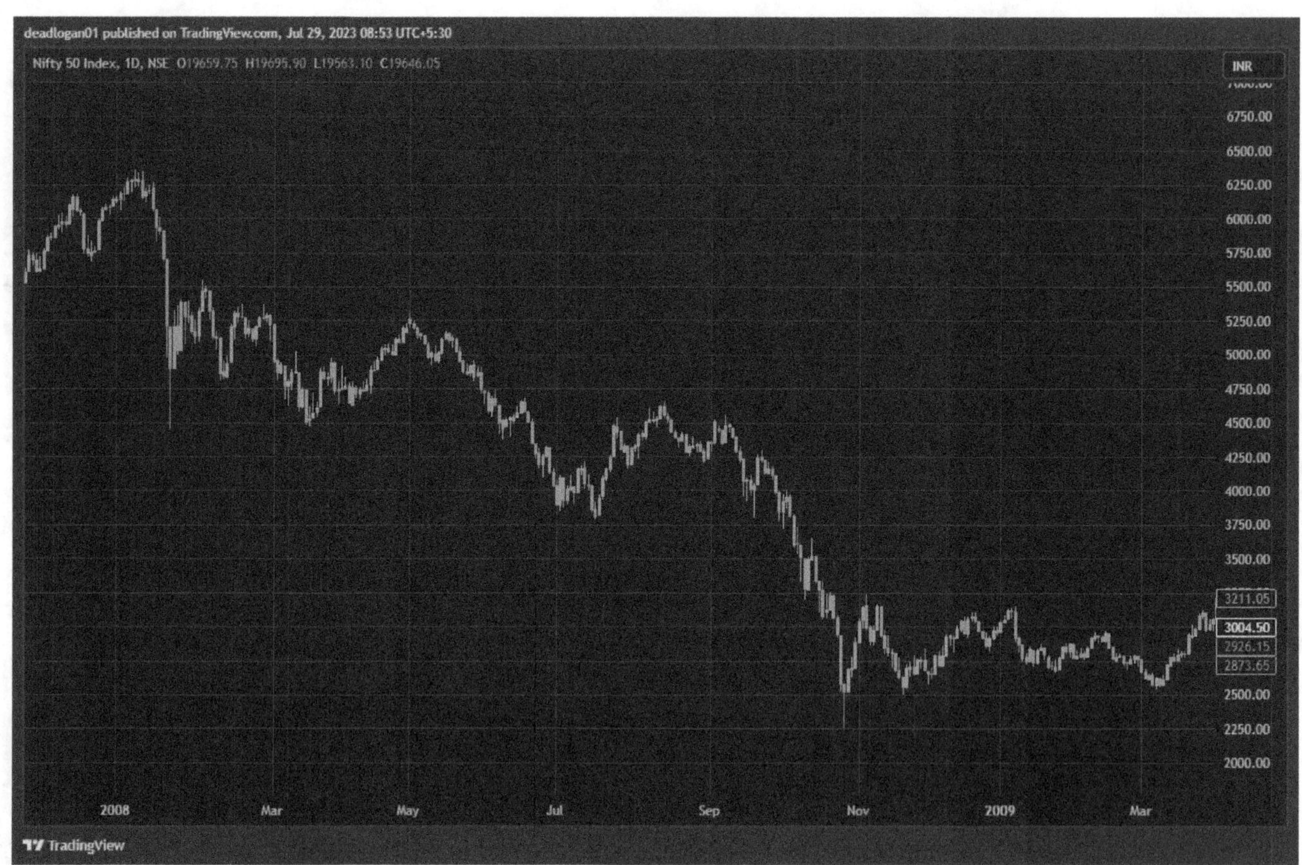

Image 1.5.3: Chart of NIFTY 50 showing the Bear Run/Economy Collapse during *"The Global Financial Crisis"*

Studying these historical events can provide valuable insights into the cyclicality of the stock market and the potential consequences of market extremes.

1.6 Strategies for Navigating Bulls and Bears:

Navigating market cycles requires strategic thinking and adaptability. Here are some essential strategies to consider:

a. Asset Allocation: Diversify your investments across different asset classes, such as stocks, bonds, and cash, to spread risk and enhance portfolio stability.

b. Dollar-Cost Averaging: Invest a fixed amount regularly over time, regardless of market conditions. This approach helps reduce the impact of market volatility on your overall portfolio.

c. Long-Term Perspective: Adopt a long-term investment horizon and resist making impulsive decisions based on short-term market fluctuations.

d. Stay Informed: Keep abreast of economic news, market trends, and company performance to make well-informed investment choices.

Conclusion:

Understanding the dynamics of bulls and bears is fundamental for any investor seeking success in the stock market. By comprehending the characteristics of these market cycles and the factors influencing their transitions, you'll be better equipped to navigate through both prosperous and challenging times. Remember, successful investing requires discipline, knowledge, and a clear understanding of your financial goals. Armed with this knowledge, you can proceed with confidence in your investment journey.

Chapter 2:
The Psychology of Investing: Overcoming Emotional Biases

Introduction:

In Chapter 1, we explored the fundamental concepts of bull and bear markets. Now, in Chapter 2, we will delve into the fascinating world of investor psychology. The decisions we make as investors are not purely rational; they are deeply influenced by emotions and cognitive biases. Understanding these psychological factors is essential for achieving success in the stock market. In this chapter, we will explore the common emotional biases that affect investors and learn strategies to overcome them.

2.1 Emotions in Investing:

Investing is a journey filled with emotions. Fear, greed, hope, and regret are just a few of the emotions that can impact our investment decisions. We will examine how emotions can lead to impulsive actions and affect our ability to make sound investment choices.

2.2 Common Emotional Biases:

In this section, we will explore some of the most common emotional biases that investors encounter:

a. Loss Aversion: The fear of losses can cause investors to be overly cautious or reluctant to sell losing investments, leading to holding onto declining assets in the hope of a rebound.

b. Confirmation Bias: Investors tend to seek out information that confirms their existing beliefs, even if it may not be accurate, leading to a biased view of investments.

c. Herd Mentality: The tendency to follow the crowd and make investment decisions based on what others are doing, rather than conducting individual research.

d. Overconfidence: Investors may overestimate their abilities and take on more risk than they can handle, leading to potential losses.

e. Anchoring: The tendency to rely heavily on the first piece of information received when making decisions, even if it is not relevant or accurate.

2.3 The Impact of Cognitive Biases:

Cognitive biases are inherent mental shortcuts that can lead to irrational decisions. We will explore how these biases influence our perceptions and judgment, often leading to suboptimal investment choices.

2.4 Avoiding Emotional Decision-making:

To overcome emotional biases, it is essential to develop a disciplined approach to investing. We will discuss several strategies to help investors make rational decisions:

a. Set Clear Investment Goals: Defining specific financial goals and timeframes can help investors stay focused on their long-term objectives.

b. Create a Diversified Portfolio: Diversification spreads risk across different assets, reducing the impact of individual investment outcomes.

c. Conduct Thorough Research: Base investment decisions on objective research and data rather than emotions or market noise.

d. Develop an Investment Plan: A well-thought-out investment plan can serve as a guide during turbulent market conditions, preventing impulsive actions.

e. Stick to a Long-term Perspective: Adopt a patient outlook and avoid making snap decisions based on short-term market fluctuations.

2.5 The Role of Financial Advisors:

Financial advisors play a crucial role in guiding investors through emotional hurdles. We will discuss how professional advice can help investors navigate the complexities of the stock market and keep emotions in check.

2.6 Psychological Resilience:

Building psychological resilience is vital for maintaining a steady course in investing. We will explore techniques and practices to develop resilience, such as mindfulness, self-awareness, and staying focused on the big picture.

Conclusion:

Emotional biases are an integral part of human nature, and they can significantly impact investment decisions. As investors, recognizing these biases and understanding how emotions influence our actions is essential for achieving success in the stock market. By adopting disciplined strategies, conducting thorough research, and seeking professional guidance, we can overcome emotional hurdles and make rational choices that align with our financial goals.

Chapter 3:
Stock Market Fundamentals: How the Market Works

Introduction:

In Chapter 2, we explored the importance of understanding investor psychology and how emotions can impact investment decisions. In Chapter 3, we will shift our focus to the fundamental workings of the stock market. Knowledge of these foundational concepts is crucial for any investor seeking success in the stock market. This chapter will cover the essential elements that drive the stock market and influence stock prices, providing you with a solid understanding of its mechanics.

3.1 What is the Stock Market?

The stock market is a vital component of the global financial system, serving as a platform where investors buy and sell ownership stakes in publicly-traded companies. It is a marketplace where stocks and other securities are traded, enabling businesses to raise capital and investors to potentially grow their wealth.

At its core, the stock market is a network of exchanges, where stocks and securities are listed and traded electronically. Investors, both individual and institutional, can participate in the stock market to buy shares of companies they believe will perform well and sell shares they no longer wish to hold.

The stock market provides companies with an opportunity to raise funds for expansion, research, or new ventures by selling ownership shares (stocks) to the public through an initial public offering (IPO). Once a company's stock is publicly traded, it can be bought and sold on the secondary market by investors.

3.2 Stock Exchanges and Trading:

Stock exchanges are central to the functioning of the stock market. These exchanges are organized marketplaces where stocks and other securities are bought and sold according to specific rules and regulations.

Key stock exchanges worldwide include:

New York Stock Exchange (NYSE): One of the largest and most well-known stock exchanges, located in New York City, USA.

NASDAQ: An electronic exchange known for listing many technology and growth-oriented companies.

London Stock Exchange (LSE): The primary stock exchange in the UK, housing various international companies.

Tokyo Stock Exchange (TSE): The principal stock exchange in Japan, featuring numerous Japanese corporations.

Bombay Stock Exchange (BSE): Asia's first exchange and the largest securities market in India.

National Stock Exchange (NSE): The first exchange in India to implement electronic or screen-based trading.

When investors buy or sell stocks, their orders are executed on these exchanges through brokerage firms or trading platforms. The trading process involves matching buyers' and sellers' orders to facilitate transactions

3.3 The Role of Stocks:

Stocks, also known as shares or equities, represent ownership in a company. When an individual or institution buys a stock, they become a shareholder and own a portion of the company's assets and profits.

As a shareholder, an investor can potentially benefit from the company's growth and profitability. This benefit comes in the form of dividends, which are a share of the company's profits distributed to shareholders, and capital appreciation, where the stock's price increases, allowing investors to sell their shares at a higher price than what they paid.

3.4 Understanding Market Participants:

The stock market is composed of a diverse group of market participants. These participants include:

Individual Investors: Individuals who invest their personal funds in the stock market, seeking to grow their wealth over time.

Institutional Investors: Large organizations, such as pension funds, mutual funds, and insurance companies that manage funds on behalf of their clients or beneficiaries.

Hedge Funds: Investment funds that employ various strategies to generate returns for their investors, often seeking to outperform the market.

Mutual Funds: Pooled funds managed by professional portfolio managers, offering investors diversification and professional management.

Each type of market participant contributes to the liquidity and efficiency of the stock market.

3.5 Market Indexes:

Market indexes play a crucial role in gauging the overall performance of the stock market. These indexes are composed of a representative selection of stocks that reflect the performance of a particular market segment or the entire market.

Prominent market indexes include:

S&P 500: A widely followed index that tracks the 500 largest publicly traded companies in the US, representing about 80% of the total US market capitalization.

Dow Jones Industrial Average (DJIA): Comprising 30 large, publicly-traded companies, this index provides insights into the overall health of the US economy.

Nasdaq Composite: A broad-based index covering all the companies listed on the NASDAQ exchange, with a focus on technology and growth stocks.

BSE Sensex: The Bombay Stock Exchange (BSE) Sensex is one of the most widely followed stock market indices in India. It consists of the 30 largest and most actively traded stocks listed on the BSE. The Sensex provides an indication of the overall performance of the Indian equity market.

NSE Nifty 50: The National Stock Exchange (NSE) Nifty 50 is another key stock market index in India. It comprises the 50 largest and most liquid stocks listed on the NSE across various sectors. The Nifty 50 is considered a broader representation of the Indian stock market compared to the Sensex.

BSE 500: The BSE 500 is a broader index that includes the top 500 companies listed on the BSE based on market capitalization. It provides a more comprehensive view of the Indian equity market, including mid-cap and small-cap stocks.

BSE Midcap and BSE Smallcap: These are separate indices that track the performance of mid-cap and small-cap companies listed on the BSE. They are considered as indicators of the performance of mid-sized and smaller companies in the Indian stock market.

NSE Bank Nifty: The NSE Bank Nifty is a sector-specific index that represents the performance of the banking sector in India. It consists of the most liquid and large banking stocks listed on the NSE.

Market indexes serve as benchmarks for investors to assess the performance of their portfolios and compare their returns to the overall market.

3.6 Factors Influencing Stock Prices:

The stock market is influenced by various factors that impact stock prices. Some key factors include:

Supply and Demand: The basic principle of supply and demand determines stock prices. When more investors want to buy a stock (demand) than sell it (supply), the price tends to rise, and vice versa.

Company Performance: The financial performance and profitability of a company directly impact its stock price. Strong earnings and revenue growth often lead to higher stock prices.

Economic Indicators: Economic indicators, such as GDP growth, unemployment rates, and inflation, can affect investor sentiment and stock market movements.

Market Sentiment: Investors' overall outlook on the market and the economy can influence their willingness to buy or sell stocks, creating shifts in stock prices.

3.7 Market Orders and Types of Orders:

When investors place orders to buy or sell stocks, they can choose from various types of orders:

Market Order: A market order instructs the broker to execute the trade at the best available price in the market. It ensures the immediate execution of the order.

Limit Order: A limit order specifies the maximum price a buyer is willing to pay or the minimum price a seller is willing to accept. It allows investors to control the price at which their order is executed.

Stop Order: A stop order becomes a market order once the stock reaches a specified price, known as the stop price. It is used to limit losses or protect profits.

Stop-Limit Order: A stop-limit order combines the features of a stop order and a limit order. It becomes a limit order once the stock reaches the stop price, but the price at which the trade is executed is limited within a specific range.

The choice of order type depends on an investor's trading strategy and risk tolerance.

3.8 Bull vs. Bear Markets and Trends:

As discussed in Chapter 1, bull and bear markets represent the prevailing market sentiment and trends:

Bull Market: A bull market is characterized by rising stock prices and positive investor sentiment. It generally reflects an optimistic outlook on the economy and corporate earnings.

Bear Market: A bear market is marked by falling stock prices and negative investor sentiment. It typically indicates a pessimistic view of the economy and corporate performance.

Understanding these market trends helps investors make informed decisions and adjust their investment strategies accordingly.

3.9 Volatility and Market Fluctuations:

Volatility refers to the degree of price fluctuations in the stock market. It is a natural characteristic of the market and can be influenced by various factors, including economic events, geopolitical developments, and unexpected news. Investors should be prepared for market fluctuations and have a risk management strategy in place to navigate volatile periods.

3.10 The Role of Market Regulators:

To ensure a fair and transparent market, various regulatory bodies oversee the stock market. These regulators establish rules and regulations to protect investors and maintain market integrity.

In INDIA, the Securities and Exchange Board of India (SEBI) is the primary regulatory authority overseeing the securities industry and enforcing securities laws.

3.11 Market Efficiency and Information:

The concept of market efficiency suggests that stock prices fully reflect all available information. According to the efficient market hypothesis, it is challenging to consistently outperform the market because stock prices quickly adjust to new information.

Investors seeking to outperform the market must conduct thorough research and analysis to identify mispriced securities or opportunities.

Conclusion:

Chapter 3 has provided a comprehensive overview of the stock market's fundamental aspects. By understanding the workings of the stock market, the role of stocks, market participants, market indexes, and the factors influencing stock prices, you are better equipped to navigate this dynamic financial landscape. In the following chapters, we will continue to explore essential concepts, investment strategies, and risk management techniques, empowering you to make well-informed decisions and pursue your financial goals in the stock market.

Chapter 4: Investment Strategies and Approaches

Introduction:

In Chapter 4, we will delve into various investment strategies and approaches that can help investors achieve their financial goals in the dynamic stock market. Each strategy possesses unique characteristics, risk profiles, and potential rewards. Understanding these approaches will empower you to tailor your investment plan according to your risk tolerance, investment objectives, and time horizon, ultimately leading you towards stock market success.

4.1 Long-term Investing:

Long-term investing is a fundamental approach where investors buy and hold stocks for an extended period, often measured in years or even decades. This strategy relies on the power of compounding returns, allowing investments to grow steadily over time. The key benefits of long-term investing include reduced transaction costs and tax advantages due to longer holding periods. By focusing on the long term, investors can ride out short-term market fluctuations and potentially benefit from the overall growth of the market.

Successful long-term investing strategies involve identifying companies with strong fundamentals and competitive advantages. Investors look for businesses with sustainable revenue growth, healthy profit margins, strong management teams, and a history of generating consistent returns for shareholders. Patience and discipline are essential virtues for long-term investors, as they avoid making impulsive decisions based on short-term market volatility.

4.2 Value Investing:

Value investing is a strategy popularized by legendary investor Warren Buffett. It involves seeking stocks that are trading at prices below their intrinsic value. In other words, value investors look for stocks they believe are undervalued by the market. The underlying philosophy is that over time, the market will recognize the true worth of these stocks, leading to price appreciation.

To practice value investing, investors conduct thorough fundamental analysis of companies, examining financial statements, competitive positioning, industry trends, and future growth prospects. The goal is to identify stocks that are trading at a discount relative to their true worth, based on intrinsic metrics like price-to-earnings (P/E) ratio, price-to-book (P/B) ratio, and other valuation measures.

4.3 Growth Investing:

Growth investing centers on identifying companies with strong potential for above-average future growth in revenue and earnings. Growth investors focus on businesses operating in rapidly expanding industries or demonstrating disruptive innovation.

Growth indicators such as sales growth rates, earnings forecasts, and market share gains are critical factors considered by growth investors. This strategy often involves paying a premium for high-growth stocks, as investors anticipate future value creation and price appreciation.

Investing in growth stocks can be rewarding, but it comes with higher volatility and risks, as these stocks can be sensitive to changes in investor sentiment and market conditions. Successful growth investors have a keen eye for companies with sustainable growth prospects and an ability to weather market fluctuations.

4.4 Dividend Investing:

Dividend investing involves seeking stocks that offer regular dividend payments to shareholders. Dividends are cash distributions made by companies to reward shareholders for their ownership. This strategy is popular among income-focused investors, such as retirees or those seeking a steady stream of passive income.

Dividend investing provides a way to generate returns even in a sideways or bearish market, as dividends can contribute significantly to the overall returns of an investment. Dividend-paying companies tend to be more mature and financially stable, as they share a portion of their profits with shareholders.

Investors in dividend stocks often prioritize companies with a history of consistent dividend payments, strong cash flows, and reasonable dividend payout ratios. Additionally, they may consider companies with a track record of increasing dividends over time, known as dividend growth stocks.

4.5 Income Investing:

Income investing is geared towards generating a steady stream of income from investments. In addition to dividend-paying stocks, income investors consider other income-generating assets such as bonds, preferred stocks, real estate investment trusts (REITs), and high-yield corporate debt.

Income investments typically have lower volatility compared to growth stocks and can serve as a source of stable cash flow for investors seeking regular income. Income investing can be particularly appealing in low-interest-rate environments, as it provides an alternative to traditional fixed-income investments.

It is essential for income investors to evaluate the credit quality of income-generating assets, as higher yields often come with increased credit risk. Diversification and risk management play crucial roles in income investing to preserve capital and ensure a sustainable income stream.

4.6 Index Investing and ETFs:

Index investing involves buying a diversified portfolio of stocks that replicate the performance of a market index, such as the S&P 500 or the Nasdaq Composite. Investors can achieve index exposure through exchange-traded funds (ETFs) or index mutual funds.

Index investing is a passive approach that aims to match the returns of the overall market or a specific market segment. This strategy is favored for its low costs, broad market exposure, and simplicity. Index investors believe that over the long term, the market tends to rise, and investing in the entire market offers a higher probability of positive returns.

ETFs are a popular vehicle for index investing, providing liquidity, real-time pricing, and the ability to trade throughout the trading day. Investors can choose from a wide range of ETFs that track various market indexes, industry sectors, or asset classes.

4.7 Sector Rotation:

Sector rotation is an active investment strategy that involves shifting investments among different industry sectors based on their economic outlook and cyclical trends. Investors use sector rotation to capitalize on changing business cycles and economic conditions.

Different sectors perform differently at different stages of the economic cycle. For example, during economic expansions, sectors like technology, consumer discretionary, and industrials tend to perform well. In contrast, defensive sectors like utilities and consumer staples may outperform during economic downturns.

Sector rotation requires research and analysis to identify the prevailing economic conditions and determine which sectors are likely to outperform or underperform. Investors need to closely monitor economic indicators, interest rates, inflation rates, and geopolitical events that can impact sector performance.

4.8 Contrarian Investing:

Contrarian investing involves going against prevailing market sentiments and making investment decisions that are opposite to the consensus. Contrarians believe that markets are influenced by emotions and can become overbought or oversold due to fear or greed.

Contrarian investors often buy stocks that are undervalued or unpopular, anticipating a reversal in market sentiment that will lead to price appreciation. Similarly, they may sell stocks that are overvalued or overly popular, expecting a correction in prices.

Contrarian investing requires conviction and patience, as it can take time for the market to recognize the underlying value of contrarian positions. This strategy can be highly rewarding but also involves higher risks, as going against the prevailing market sentiment can be challenging.

4.9 Technical Analysis:

Technical analysis involves analyzing historical price and volume data to forecast future stock price movements. This approach relies on chart patterns, technical indicators, and trend analysis to identify potential entry and exit points for trades.

Technical analysts believe that historical price patterns repeat themselves due to human behavior in the market. They use chart patterns like head and shoulders, double tops and bottoms, and moving averages to spot trends and potential price reversals.

Technical analysis can be particularly useful for short-term traders and investors who seek to profit from short-term market movements. However, it has its limitations, as it does not consider a company's fundamentals or intrinsic value.

4.10 Fundamental Analysis:

Fundamental analysis focuses on evaluating the intrinsic value of a company by examining its financial health, management quality, competitive advantage, and growth prospects. Fundamental analysts assess factors like earnings per share, revenue growth, profit margins, and debt levels to determine a company's true worth.

By comparing a company's intrinsic value with its current stock price, fundamental analysts can identify undervalued or overvalued stocks. This approach helps investors make informed decisions based on a company's fundamentals rather than short-term market fluctuations.

Fundamental analysis is often used by long-term investors and value investors to identify stocks with solid growth potential and strong financials. It requires a deep understanding of financial statements, industry dynamics, and macroeconomic factors that can impact a company's performance.

4.11 Risk Management:

No investment strategy is complete without a robust risk management plan. Risk management involves strategies to protect capital, minimize losses, and diversify investments to reduce overall risk.

Diversification is a fundamental risk management technique that involves spreading investments across different assets, industries, and geographies.

Diversified portfolios can mitigate the impact of adverse market movements in any particular asset or sector.

Setting stop-loss orders is another risk management practice used by investors to limit losses on individual positions. Stop-loss orders trigger the sale of a security when it reaches a predefined price level, preventing further losses in a declining market.

Asset allocation is another critical component of risk management. Investors determine the allocation of their portfolio among various asset classes, such as stocks, bonds, cash, and alternative investments, based on their risk tolerance and investment objectives.

Conclusion:

Chapter 4 has provided an in-depth exploration of various investment strategies and approaches available to investors in the stock market. Each strategy offers unique benefits and challenges, and the most suitable approach will depend on individual preferences and financial goals.

As you progress through this book, consider which strategies resonate with you and align best with your investment objectives. Developing a well-rounded investment plan that combines multiple strategies can help you navigate the dynamic stock market successfully.

Remember that no investment strategy is entirely risk-free, and it is crucial to understand the risks associated with each approach. Continuously educate yourself, stay informed about market trends, and be prepared to adapt your investment strategy as market conditions change.

The subsequent chapters will further build on this knowledge, equipping you with the tools and insights needed to make informed investment decisions and achieve stock market success.

Chapter 5:
Risk Management in Stock Market Investing

Introduction:

In Chapter 5, we will delve into the critical aspect of risk management in stock market investing. While investing in the stock market can be rewarding, it also involves inherent risks. Understanding and effectively managing these risks are essential for preserving capital, achieving long-term financial goals, and navigating the ups and downs of the market. This chapter will equip you with valuable strategies and techniques to identify, assess, and mitigate various types of risks associated with stock market investing.

5.1 Types of Risks in Stock Market Investing:

In this section, we will explore the different types of risks investors encounter in the stock market. These risks include:

Market Risk: Also known as systematic risk, it refers to the overall volatility of the market that affects all investments.

Company-Specific Risk: Unique risks associated with individual companies, such as management changes or product failures.

Systemic Risk: The risk of a widespread financial system collapse, such as a global economic crisis.

Currency Risk: The risk of currency fluctuations when investing in foreign markets or holding assets denominated in different currencies.

Interest Rate Risk: The risk that changes in interest rates can impact the value of fixed-income investments.

Liquidity Risk: The risk of not being able to buy or sell an asset quickly at a fair price due to insufficient market liquidity.

Regulatory Risk: The risk arising from changes in laws and regulations that may impact investments.

Understanding each type of risk will lay the groundwork for formulating a comprehensive risk management plan.

5.2 Risk Tolerance and Investment Objectives:

Assessing your risk tolerance and defining investment objectives is a fundamental step in risk management. We will discuss how risk tolerance varies among individuals and how it influences investment decisions. Investors with a higher risk tolerance may be more comfortable with volatile assets, while those with a lower risk tolerance may prefer more stable investments. Additionally, we will explore how clearly defined investment objectives guide risk management decisions tailored to specific financial goals.

5.3 Diversification:

Diversification is one of the most effective risk management strategies. This section will delve into the concept of diversification and how it helps reduce risk in a portfolio. By spreading investments across different asset classes, industries, and geographic regions, investors can lower the impact of adverse market movements on any specific investment. We will discuss how diversification improves risk-adjusted returns and provides a more balanced investment approach.

5.4 Asset Allocation:

Asset allocation is a crucial component of risk management, determining the allocation of a portfolio among different asset classes based on risk profiles and investment objectives. We will explore various asset allocation strategies, ranging from aggressive growth portfolios to conservative income-focused portfolios. The goal is to align asset allocation with an investor's risk tolerance and time horizon.

5.5 Risk-Return Tradeoff:

Understanding the risk-return tradeoff is essential for making informed investment decisions. We will explain the relationship between risk and potential returns, with higher-risk investments offering the potential for higher rewards, but also carrying higher chances of losses. Balancing risk and return is crucial in constructing a well-rounded investment portfolio that aligns with an individual's financial goals.

5.6 Stop-Loss Orders:

Stop-loss orders are valuable risk management tools that investors can use to limit potential losses. In this section, we will explore how stop-loss orders work, different types of stop-loss orders, and how to determine appropriate levels for setting these orders based on individual risk tolerance and market conditions. Stop-loss orders can help protect capital and prevent emotional decision-making in volatile markets.

5.7 Hedging Strategies:

Hedging strategies are used to protect against potential adverse price movements in specific investments or the overall market. We will discuss various hedging techniques, including options, futures contracts, and inverse exchange-traded funds (ETFs). Understanding these strategies will enable investors to use hedging as an additional layer of protection in their investment portfolio.

5.8 Risk Management for Different Investment Styles:

Different investment styles, such as value investing, growth investing, and income investing, carry varying levels of risk. This section will explore risk management approaches tailored to each investment style. Understanding the risks inherent in different investment strategies will help investors make informed decisions while aligning their portfolio with their preferred investment approach.

5.9 Risk Management for International Investments:

Investing in international markets introduces additional risks, such as currency risk, geopolitical risk, and regulatory differences. This section will discuss risk management strategies specific to international investments and how to evaluate the risks and potential rewards of investing in foreign markets.

5.10 Monitoring and Reviewing Your Portfolio:

Continuously monitoring and reviewing your investment portfolio is crucial for effective risk management. This section emphasizes the importance of regular portfolio reviews, including rebalancing and adjusting asset allocation to align with changing market conditions and investment objectives. Staying proactive and responsive to market changes is key to maintaining a well-managed portfolio.

Conclusion:

Chapter 5 has provided a comprehensive exploration of risk management in stock market investing. Understanding different types of risks, assessing risk tolerance and investment objectives, and employing effective risk management strategies are essential for achieving long-term success as an investor.

By incorporating risk management principles into your investment approach, you can build a resilient portfolio that aligns with your financial goals and withstands various market conditions. In the subsequent chapters, we will further deepen our understanding of stock market investing, exploring advanced investment techniques, market analysis, and the role of psychology in investment decision-making. Armed with comprehensive knowledge and sound risk management practices, you will be better equipped to navigate the stock market confidently and achieve your financial aspirations.

Chapter 6:
Fundamental Analysis - Evaluating Company Performance

Introduction:

Chapter 6 explores fundamental analysis, a critical approach to evaluating company performance and determining the intrinsic value of stocks. Fundamental analysis involves assessing a company's financial health, competitive position, management quality, growth prospects, and overall potential for generating value for shareholders. By understanding fundamental analysis, investors can make informed investment decisions based on a company's underlying strengths and weaknesses, rather than short-term market sentiment.

6.1 The Importance of Fundamental Analysis:

Fundamental analysis is the cornerstone of sound stock market investing. This section emphasizes its importance in providing a comprehensive understanding of a company's financial health and intrinsic value. By analyzing a company's fundamentals, investors can gain insights into its long-term growth potential, stability, and ability to generate sustainable profits. Unlike short-term trading, fundamental analysis focuses on a company's fundamentals over an extended period, guiding investors towards stocks with solid long-term prospects.

6.2 Financial Statements and Ratios: To perform fundamental analysis, investors must understand a company's financial statements. This section explores the three primary financial statements:

Income Statement: It provides a summary of a company's revenues, expenses, and profits over a specific period. Key metrics include revenue, gross profit, operating profit, net profit, and earnings per share (EPS).

Balance Sheet: It presents a snapshot of a company's assets, liabilities, and shareholders' equity at a particular point in time. Key metrics include total assets, total liabilities, shareholders' equity, and working capital.

Cash Flow Statement: It tracks the flow of cash in and out of a company during a specific period. Key metrics include operating cash flow, investing cash flow, and financing cash flow.

Additionally, financial ratios play a crucial role in analyzing a company's performance. We will discuss key financial ratios such as price-to-earnings (P/E), price-to-book (P/B), earnings per share (EPS), return on equity (ROE), and debt-to-equity ratio. These ratios provide valuable insights into a company's profitability, liquidity, and overall financial health.

6.3 Evaluating Revenue and Profitability:

A company's revenue growth and profitability are fundamental drivers of its financial performance. This section focuses on assessing these key aspects. Investors analyze revenue trends to understand a company's ability to increase sales over time. Consistent revenue growth indicates a company's competitiveness and demand for its products or services.

Profitability analysis involves examining profit margins, such as gross profit margin and net profit margin, to assess how efficiently a company operates. A company with healthy profit margins demonstrates its ability to control costs and generate profits from its core operations.

6.4 Management and Corporate Governance:

The quality of a company's management team and its corporate governance practices significantly influence its performance. This section explores how effective leadership, vision, and decision-making can drive a company's success. Investors evaluate a company's management track record, industry expertise, and strategic planning capabilities to assess the team's ability to navigate challenges and capitalize on opportunities.

Corporate governance practices, such as transparent financial reporting and shareholder-friendly policies, are crucial in fostering investor confidence. Companies with strong corporate governance frameworks are more likely to act in the best interests of shareholders.

6.5 Competitive Advantage and Moat:

A company's competitive advantage, often referred to as its "moat," is a crucial concept in fundamental analysis. This section discusses different types of competitive advantages that companies can possess, such as:

Brand Strength: A strong and recognizable brand can attract loyal customers and support premium pricing.

Intellectual Property: Patents, trademarks, and copyrights can provide companies with a unique market position and barriers to entry for competitors.

Economies of Scale: Larger companies may enjoy cost advantages due to lower production costs per unit.

Network Effects: Companies with network effects, like social media platforms, become more valuable as more users join the network.

Understanding a company's competitive advantage helps investors evaluate its ability to maintain profitability and fend off competition.

6.6 Growth Prospects and Industry Analysis:

Assessing a company's growth prospects and the industry it operates in is essential for fundamental analysis. This section explores how industry dynamics can impact a company's performance. Investors analyze industry trends, market potential, and technological advancements to gauge a company's growth potential.

Identifying companies in growing industries can provide attractive investment opportunities. Conversely, companies operating in declining or saturated industries may face challenges in achieving significant growth.

6.7 Valuation Techniques: Valuation is a critical aspect of fundamental analysis. This section explains various valuation techniques used to determine a company's intrinsic value. Some common valuation methods include:

Discounted Cash Flow (DCF) Analysis: This method estimates a company's future cash flows and discounts them back to present value to determine its worth.

Relative Valuation: Investors compare a company's financial ratios and performance metrics to those of its peers to assess its relative value within the industry.

The Gordon Growth Model: This model estimates a company's intrinsic value based on its dividends and expected dividend growth rate.

Valuation helps investors identify stocks that may be undervalued or overvalued compared to their intrinsic worth.

6.8 Evaluating Risk Factors:

Understanding and quantifying risk factors are essential parts of fundamental analysis. This section discusses how risks, such as market competition, regulatory changes, technological disruptions, and macroeconomic factors, can impact a company's performance. By analyzing risk factors, investors can assess a company's ability to withstand challenges and remain resilient.

6.9 Importance of Qualitative Analysis:

While financial metrics are crucial, qualitative analysis also plays a significant role in fundamental analysis. This section highlights the importance of considering qualitative factors, such as a company's corporate culture, brand reputation, innovation, and environmental, social, and governance (ESG) practices. These qualitative aspects can influence a company's long-term prospects and investor perception.

Investors use ESG criteria to evaluate a company's sustainability efforts, ethical practices, and social impact. Incorporating qualitative analysis into fundamental analysis provides a more holistic view of a company's potential.

6.10 Investment Decisions based on Fundamental Analysis:

This section discusses how to make investment decisions based on fundamental analysis. Combining financial analysis, industry outlook, management quality, competitive positioning, and qualitative factors helps investors select stocks that align with their investment objectives and risk tolerance.

Fundamental analysis guides investors toward stocks with strong growth potential and attractive valuations while avoiding companies with weak financials or overvalued stocks. By integrating fundamental analysis into an overall investment strategy, investors can make well-informed and prudent decisions.

Conclusion:

Chapter 6 has provided a comprehensive exploration of fundamental analysis and its significance in stock market investing. Understanding a company's financial health, growth prospects, competitive advantage, and management quality is critical for identifying valuable investment opportunities.

As you progress through this book, consider incorporating fundamental analysis into your investment approach to make informed decisions based on a company's intrinsic value and long-term potential. In the subsequent chapters, we will further deepen our understanding of stock market investing, exploring advanced investment techniques, market analysis, and the role of psychology in investment decision-making. Armed with comprehensive knowledge and sound fundamental analysis practices, you will be better equipped to navigate the stock market with confidence and achieve your financial aspirations.

Chapter 7:
Technical Analysis - Understanding Market Trends and Patterns

Introduction:

Chapter 7 explores technical analysis, a method of evaluating stocks and financial markets based on historical price and volume data. Unlike fundamental analysis, which focuses on a company's financial health and intrinsic value, technical analysis is primarily concerned with chart patterns and market behavior. By understanding technical analysis, investors can make informed trading and investment decisions based on price patterns, market trends, and market sentiment.

7.1 The Foundations of Technical Analysis:

To lay the groundwork for technical analysis, this section introduces fundamental concepts and principles that underpin the approach. Investors will learn about key elements such as support and resistance levels, trendlines, and moving averages. These foundational tools are crucial for interpreting price charts and identifying potential trading opportunities.

Support and resistance levels represent key price levels where the price has historically reversed or stalled. Support acts as a price floor, preventing the stock from falling further, while resistance acts as a price ceiling, preventing the stock from rising higher. Understanding these levels helps investors set entry and exit points for their trades.

Trendlines are lines drawn on a price chart to connect consecutive highs or lows, helping to identify the overall direction of the market or an individual stock's price. Trendlines provide insights into uptrends, downtrends, and sideways trends.

Moving averages are technical indicators that smooth out price data and reveal underlying trends. Different types of moving averages, such as simple moving averages (SMA) and exponential moving averages (EMA), help traders identify potential trend changes and spot support and resistance levels.

7.2 Price Charts and Timeframes:

Technical analysis relies heavily on price charts to visualize historical price movements. This section explores various types of price charts, including line charts, bar charts, and candlestick charts. Each chart type provides a different perspective on price movements, helping investors choose the most suitable chart for their analysis.

Additionally, investors will learn about different timeframes, such as daily, weekly, and intraday charts. Choosing the appropriate timeframe is essential, as it affects the accuracy and relevance of the analysis. Short-term traders may prefer intraday charts, while long-term investors may focus on weekly or monthly charts.

7.3 Trend Analysis:

Identifying trends is a fundamental aspect of technical analysis. This section delves deeper into trend analysis, discussing various methods to recognize uptrends, downtrends, and sideways trends. Trend analysis helps investors understand the prevailing direction of the market or a specific stock, which is crucial for making timely trading decisions.

When analyzing trends, investors will learn to identify higher highs and higher lows in uptrends, lower highs and lower lows in downtrends, and relatively equal highs and lows in sideways trends.

7.4 Chart Patterns:

Chart patterns are recurring formations on price charts that provide valuable insights into potential future price movements. This section covers some of the most common chart patterns that technical analysts use to make predictions:

Head and Shoulders: A pattern with three peaks, where the middle peak (the head) is higher than the two surrounding peaks (the shoulders). It often signals a potential trend reversal from bullish to bearish.

Double Tops and Double Bottoms: Two price peaks (tops) or troughs (bottoms) that are relatively equal in height, indicating potential trend reversals.

Triangles (Ascending, Descending, Symmetrical): Triangle-shaped patterns that show a potential consolidation phase before a significant price movement.

Flags and Pennants: Short-term continuation patterns that form after a sharp price movement, signaling a brief pause before the trend continues.

Cup and Handle: A bullish continuation pattern consisting of a rounded bottom (the cup) followed by a smaller price consolidation (the handle).

__Wedges (Rising and Falling):__ Patterns characterized by converging trendlines, indicating a potential price breakout in the direction of the wedge.

Recognizing these chart patterns helps investors anticipate potential price movements and plan their trades accordingly.

7.5 Support and Resistance:

Support and resistance levels are essential concepts in technical analysis. This section provides a more detailed understanding of how to identify and interpret support and resistance levels on price charts. Investors will learn how to use these levels to set stop-loss orders and determine potential price targets.

Support levels act as buying zones where demand for the stock is strong enough to prevent further price declines. When the price reaches a support level, it tends to rebound. Resistance levels, on the other hand, act as selling zones where supply exceeds demand, causing the price to stall or reverse.

7.6 Moving Averages:

Moving averages are widely used technical indicators that help traders identify trends and potential entry and exit points. This section explores various types of moving averages, such as simple moving averages (SMA) and exponential moving averages (EMA). Investors will learn how to interpret moving average crossovers, where short-term and long-term moving averages intersect, to identify potential trend changes.

Moving averages can also serve as dynamic support and resistance levels, helping traders gauge the stock's current trend and potential areas of reversal.

7.7 Oscillators and Indicators:

Oscillators and technical indicators are tools that help traders gauge market momentum and overbought or oversold conditions. This section delves into popular oscillators, including the Relative Strength Index (RSI), Moving Average Convergence Divergence (MACD), and Stochastic Oscillator.

These indicators help investors identify potential trend reversals, overbought or oversold conditions, and divergences between price and momentum, which can signal potential market turning points.

7.8 Volume Analysis:

Volume is an essential component of technical analysis, providing insights into the strength of price movements. This section explains how to analyze volume data on price charts and how to use volume indicators, such as the On-Balance Volume (OBV), to confirm price trends and identify potential reversals.

When volume increases significantly during a price move, it suggests strong market participation and conviction, making the price movement more reliable.

7.9 Fibonacci Retracements and Extensions:

Fibonacci retracements and extensions are based on mathematical ratios and are used to identify potential support and resistance levels. This section delves into the concept of the Fibonacci sequence and how traders apply Fibonacci levels on price charts.

Fibonacci retracements help identify potential levels where the price may retrace before continuing in the direction of the trend. Fibonacci extensions provide insights into potential price targets during a strong trend.

7.10 Technical Analysis Strategies:

This section explores various technical analysis strategies used by traders and investors. Traders often use trend-following techniques, where they enter positions in the direction of the prevailing trend. Breakout trading involves entering positions when the price breaks through significant support or resistance levels.

Momentum trading focuses on securities with strong price momentum, while mean reversion strategies capitalize on price movements that revert to the mean.

7.11 Integrating Fundamental and Technical Analysis:

While fundamental and technical analysis are distinct approaches, some investors prefer to combine both methods for a more comprehensive view of the market. This section discusses how to integrate fundamental and technical analysis to make well-informed investment decisions.

By combining the insights gained from fundamental analysis (e.g., company financials, growth prospects) with technical analysis (e.g., chart patterns, trend analysis), investors can create a more robust investment strategy.

Conclusion:

Chapter 7 has provided a comprehensive exploration of technical analysis and its significance in stock market investing. Understanding chart patterns, trend analysis, technical indicators, and other technical tools can help investors identify potential trading opportunities and manage risk.

As you progress through this book, consider incorporating technical analysis into your investment approach to complement fundamental analysis and make well-rounded investment decisions. In the subsequent chapters, we will further deepen our understanding of stock market investing, exploring advanced investment techniques, market analysis, and the role of psychology in investment decision-making. Armed with comprehensive knowledge and a well-rounded analytical approach, you will be better equipped to navigate the stock market with confidence and achieve your financial aspirations.

Chapter 8:
Risk Management and Portfolio Diversification

Introduction:

Chapter 8 focuses on two crucial aspects of successful stock market investing: risk management and portfolio diversification. These practices are essential for protecting capital, minimizing potential losses, and achieving long-term investment goals. Understanding risk management and portfolio diversification empowers investors to make informed decisions, reduce exposure to market volatility, and build resilient investment portfolios.

8.1 Understanding Investment Risk:

Investment risk refers to the possibility of experiencing losses or lower-than-expected returns due to various factors affecting the financial markets. There are different types of risk that investors should be aware of:

Market Risk: Also known as systematic risk, it is the risk of losses resulting from overall market movements, such as changes in interest rates, economic conditions, or geopolitical events. Market risk affects all investments to some extent and cannot be eliminated through diversification.

Credit Risk: This risk pertains to the potential of a borrower (company, government, or individual) failing to meet its debt obligations, leading to a decline in the value of the related securities, such as bonds.

Liquidity Risk: Liquidity risk arises when investors are unable to buy or sell an asset quickly and at a reasonable price due to limited market activity or large bid-ask spreads. Illiquid assets can be challenging to exit during market downturns.

Inflation Risk: Inflation risk refers to the erosion of purchasing power over time due to rising prices. If the rate of inflation outpaces the return on investments, the real value of the investment decreases.

Understanding different types of risk allows investors to evaluate the potential risks associated with their investments and make appropriate risk management decisions.

8.2 Assessing Risk Tolerance:

Risk tolerance is an individual's ability and willingness to endure fluctuations in the value of their investments. It is influenced by various factors, including financial circumstances, investment goals, time horizon, and emotional capacity to handle market volatility.

Investors can assess their risk tolerance through questionnaires or discussions with financial advisors. A conservative investor may have a low risk tolerance and prefer stable, income-generating investments, while an aggressive investor may have a higher risk tolerance and be comfortable with more volatile, growth-oriented assets.

8.3 Setting Investment Goals:

Establishing clear investment goals is a critical step in risk management and portfolio construction. Investors should define their objectives, such as capital preservation, wealth accumulation, retirement planning, or funding specific milestones.

Different investment goals require varying levels of risk exposure. For example, long-term goals may allow for more risk-taking, while short-term goals may necessitate a more conservative approach to safeguard capital.

8.4 Diversification Benefits and Strategies:

Portfolio diversification involves spreading investments across a range of asset classes, sectors, and geographical regions. Diversification aims to reduce the overall risk of the portfolio by minimizing the impact of adverse events on any single investment.

The benefits of diversification include:

Risk Reduction: Diversifying across different assets and industries reduces the concentration of risk in any single position.

Smoother Returns: Diversification can lead to more stable portfolio performance, as losses in one area may be offset by gains in another.

Enhanced Risk-Adjusted Returns: A well-diversified portfolio can offer a better risk-return tradeoff compared to a concentrated portfolio.

To achieve diversification, investors can adopt various strategies:

Asset Allocation: Allocating funds among different asset classes, such as stocks, bonds, real estate, and cash, based on risk tolerance and investment objectives.

Sector Diversification: Spreading investments across diverse industry sectors to reduce exposure to the performance of a specific sector.

Geographical Diversification: Investing in assets from different countries and regions to reduce country-specific risks and benefit from global opportunities.

Diversification and Correlation: Considering the correlation between assets is important; assets with low correlation can provide more effective risk reduction when combined.

8.5 Risk-Return Tradeoff:

The risk-return tradeoff is a fundamental principle in investing. It states that higher potential returns are generally associated with higher levels of risk. Investors must consider this tradeoff when making investment decisions.

Higher-risk investments, such as stocks, have the potential for higher returns over the long term, but they also carry greater short-term volatility and the risk of significant losses. Lower-risk investments, like high-quality bonds, may offer more stable returns but may not provide the same long-term growth potential.

8.6 Capital Preservation and Risk Mitigation Strategies:

Capital preservation is a primary concern for investors with low risk tolerance or those nearing retirement. Implementing risk mitigation strategies is essential to safeguard capital during market downturns. Some risk mitigation strategies include:

Stop-Loss Orders: Setting predetermined price levels to automatically sell a stock when it reaches a specific price, limiting potential losses.

Hedging: Using financial instruments, like options or futures contracts, to offset potential losses in a portfolio due to adverse market movements.

Defensive Assets: Including defensive assets, such as high-quality bonds or dividend-paying stocks, in the portfolio to provide stability during market turbulence.

8.7 Monitoring and Rebalancing:

Investors should regularly monitor the performance of their portfolio and review their investment objectives and risk tolerance. Periodic rebalancing is necessary to maintain the desired asset allocation and risk exposure. Over time, the original asset allocation may drift due to varying returns of different investments. Rebalancing involves adjusting the portfolio to bring it back in line with the intended allocation.

8.8 Understanding Behavioral Biases:

Investors are often influenced by behavioral biases, which can lead to irrational decision-making. Some common biases include:

Loss Aversion: The tendency to prefer avoiding losses over making gains, which may lead to holding onto losing investments for too long.

Overconfidence: Believing one's ability to predict market movements with great accuracy, leading to excessive risk-taking.

Herd Mentality: Following the crowd and making investment decisions based on the actions of others, without conducting independent analysis.

Confirmation Bias: Seeking information that confirms pre-existing beliefs and disregarding contradictory data.

Recognizing these biases is crucial for making rational investment decisions and avoiding impulsive actions driven by emotions.

8.9 Seeking Professional Advice:

Investing can be complex, and seeking advice from financial professionals can be beneficial, especially for those new to the stock market. Financial advisors can help investors assess their risk tolerance, set realistic investment goals, and construct well-structured portfolios aligned with their objectives.

Conclusion:

Chapter 8 has explored risk management and portfolio diversification, two essential components of successful stock market investing. Understanding investment risk, assessing risk tolerance, and setting clear investment goals are fundamental in building a resilient portfolio.

By diversifying across various assets and employing risk mitigation strategies, investors can reduce vulnerability to market fluctuations. Balancing the risk-return tradeoff ensures that investment decisions align with individual risk tolerance and financial objectives.

As investors continue through this book, they should remember that risk management and portfolio diversification are ongoing processes. Regular monitoring, periodic rebalancing, and awareness of behavioral biases will help navigate the stock market confidently and work towards achieving financial goals. In the subsequent chapters, we will further deepen our understanding of stock market investing, exploring advanced investment techniques, market analysis, and the role of psychology in investment decision-making. Armed with comprehensive knowledge and prudent risk management strategies, investors will be better equipped to navigate the stock market with confidence and achieve their financial aspirations.

Chapter 9:
Advanced Investment Strategies and Market Analysis

Introduction:

Chapter 9 delves into advanced investment strategies and market analysis techniques used by experienced investors to gain a competitive edge in the stock market. These strategies go beyond the basics and require a deeper understanding of market dynamics, technical indicators, and macroeconomic factors. By mastering advanced investment strategies and market analysis, investors can enhance their decision-making process and potentially achieve superior returns.

9.1 Momentum Trading:

Momentum trading is an active trading strategy that involves buying assets that have exhibited strong recent price performance and selling assets that have shown weak performance. The underlying principle is that assets that have performed well in the past are likely to continue their trend, while underperforming assets may continue to decline.

Investors employing momentum trading strategies use technical indicators, such as Relative Strength Index (RSI) and Moving Average Convergence Divergence (MACD), to identify assets with significant price momentum. It is essential to carefully manage risk when using this strategy, as momentum can change quickly, leading to potential losses.

9.2 Contrarian Investing:

Contrarian investing is the opposite of momentum trading. It involves buying assets that are currently out of favor with the market but have the potential for a rebound. Contrarian investors believe that market sentiment can drive asset prices away from their intrinsic value, providing buying opportunities.

Contrarian investing requires strong conviction and the ability to withstand short-term market pessimism. Successful contrarians conduct thorough fundamental analysis to identify undervalued assets and potential catalysts for a turnaround.

9.3 Growth at a Reasonable Price (GARP) Investing:

GARP investing is a hybrid strategy that combines elements of both growth and value investing. GARP investors seek companies with above-average growth prospects trading at reasonable valuations.

The strategy involves identifying companies with strong earnings growth potential and evaluating their price-to-earnings (P/E) ratios relative to their growth rates. GARP investors aim to avoid overpriced growth stocks while also avoiding undervalued companies with deteriorating fundamentals.

9.4 Technical Analysis:

Advanced Chart Patterns and Indicators: Building on the foundational technical analysis concepts from Chapter 7, this section explores advanced chart patterns and technical indicators used by skilled traders and analysts.

Advanced chart patterns include:

Fibonacci Extensions: Identifying potential price targets beyond the standard Fibonacci retracement levels to forecast the extent of price movements.

Harmonic Patterns: Identifying specific geometric price patterns that suggest potential trend reversals.

Technical indicators include:

Bollinger Bands: Indicating the volatility of an asset and potential overbought or oversold conditions.

Ichimoku Cloud: Providing insights into support, resistance, and trend direction.

Parabolic SAR: Identifying potential entry and exit points based on price trends.

Utilizing advanced chart patterns and technical indicators requires a comprehensive understanding of their nuances and interpretation.

9.5 Fundamental Analysis: Advanced Techniques:

Building on the fundamental analysis concepts from previous chapters, this section explores advanced techniques used to assess a company's financial health and prospects in greater detail.

Advanced fundamental analysis techniques include:

Discounted Cash Flow (DCF) Analysis: Estimating a company's intrinsic value by forecasting its future cash flows and discounting them back to the present value.

Earnings Quality Analysis: Evaluating the sustainability and reliability of a company's earnings, ensuring they are not artificially inflated.

Scenario Analysis: Assessing a company's performance under different economic scenarios to understand its resilience to changing market conditions.

Sophisticated investors use advanced fundamental analysis techniques to make well-informed investment decisions and uncover hidden value in the market.

9.6 Sector Rotation Strategies:

Sector rotation involves shifting investments among different sectors based on their economic outlook. This advanced strategy aims to capitalize on the cyclicality of various sectors, taking advantage of sectors poised for growth while avoiding those facing headwinds.

Sophisticated investors analyze economic indicators and market trends to identify sectors with strong growth prospects. Sector rotation strategies require precise timing and a thorough understanding of macroeconomic factors.

9.7 Event-Driven Investing:

Event-driven investing involves capitalizing on specific corporate events or market developments that can impact a company's stock price. These events include mergers and acquisitions, earnings announcements, regulatory decisions, and corporate restructuring.

Investors employing event-driven strategies conduct in-depth research and analysis to assess the potential impact of specific events on a company's value and stock performance.

Conclusion:

Chapter 9 has explored advanced investment strategies and market analysis techniques employed by experienced investors to gain a competitive edge in the stock market. Momentum trading, contrarian investing, GARP investing, and sector rotation are advanced strategies that require specialized knowledge and disciplined execution.

Technical analysis using advanced chart patterns and indicators, as well as advanced fundamental analysis techniques, offer sophisticated investors deeper insights into market dynamics and potential investment opportunities.

Event-driven investing allows investors to capitalize on specific market events that can trigger significant price movements.

As investors continue through this book, they should carefully evaluate the suitability of advanced strategies based on their risk tolerance, investment goals, and level of expertise. Employing advanced investment techniques requires in-depth research, precise execution, and diligent risk management.

In the subsequent chapters, we will explore additional topics, including market analysis, psychology in investing, and the impact of macroeconomic factors on the stock market. Armed with comprehensive knowledge and a diverse set of investment strategies, investors will be better equipped to navigate the stock market with confidence and make informed decisions to achieve their financial aspirations.

Chapter 10:
Market Analysis and Macro Influences

Introduction:

Chapter 10 delves into market analysis and the macroeconomic factors that influence the stock market. Understanding market analysis helps investors make informed decisions based on the overall market environment, while considering macro influences allows them to navigate potential risks and opportunities arising from economic trends. By mastering market analysis and recognizing macroeconomic factors, investors can enhance their understanding of market dynamics and refine their investment strategies.

10.1 Market Analysis: Fundamental vs. Technical Analysis Review:

Before delving into macroeconomic influences, this section provides a comprehensive review of fundamental and technical analysis covered in previous chapters.

Fundamental Analysis: Examining a company's financial health, competitive position, and growth prospects to determine its intrinsic value. Fundamental analysis includes analyzing financial statements, earnings reports, management, and industry trends.

Technical Analysis: Analyzing historical price and volume data to identify patterns and trends, and using technical indicators to make investment decisions. Technical analysis focuses on chart patterns, trend lines, and moving averages.

By combining fundamental and technical analysis, investors gain a more comprehensive view of the market and can make well-informed investment choices.

10.2 Macroeconomic Factors Affecting the Stock Market:

Macroeconomic factors are broad economic indicators that influence the overall economy and subsequently impact the stock market. Understanding these factors is vital for assessing the market's health and making informed investment decisions. Key macroeconomic factors include:

Economic Growth: The rate at which a country's economy expands or contracts. Positive economic growth is generally associated with rising stock prices, while economic contractions may lead to market declines.

Interest Rates: The cost of borrowing money and a crucial tool used by central banks to control inflation and economic growth. Lower interest rates can stimulate borrowing and investment, potentially boosting stock prices.

Inflation: The rate at which prices of goods and services rise over time. Moderate inflation can be positive for the economy and the stock market, but high inflation erodes purchasing power and can be detrimental to stocks.

Unemployment: The percentage of the labor force that is unemployed. Low unemployment is indicative of a healthy economy and may support higher stock prices.

Consumer Spending: The total expenditures made by consumers on goods and services. Strong consumer spending can drive corporate profits and positively impact the stock market.

Government Policies: Fiscal and monetary policies enacted by governments and central banks can have significant effects on the economy and markets. Policies like tax changes, stimulus packages, and interest rate adjustments can influence investor sentiment.

Geopolitical Events: Political developments, international relations, and global conflicts can introduce uncertainty and affect investor confidence, leading to market volatility.

10.3 Business Cycles and Their Impact on Stocks:

Business cycles are recurring patterns of economic expansion and contraction. Understanding these cycles is crucial for investors as different industries and sectors perform differently during each phase:

Expansion: Economic growth, increasing consumer spending, and rising corporate profits benefit stocks, especially cyclical sectors like technology, consumer discretionary, and industrials.

Peak: Economic growth starts to slow, and investor optimism may decline. Defensive sectors like utilities, healthcare, and consumer staples tend to perform better during this phase.

Contraction: Economic activity contracts and corporate earnings decline. Defensive stocks become more attractive to investors seeking stable returns and lower risk.

Trough: Economic activity reaches its lowest point, and stocks may experience significant declines. Recovery is on the horizon, making this phase a potential opportunity for long-term investors.

Investors who understand business cycles can adjust their portfolios to capitalize on sector rotations and potential market trends.

10.4 Global Economic Trends and Market Impact:

Global economic trends, such as international trade, currency exchange rates, and global economic growth, can significantly influence the stock market. The interconnectedness of economies worldwide means that events in one country can have far-reaching effects on global markets.

Trade Relations: Tariffs, trade agreements, and trade imbalances can impact the earnings of multinational companies and sectors heavily reliant on international trade.

Currency Movements: Fluctuations in currency exchange rates can affect the profits of companies engaged in international trade and may lead to volatility in the stock market.

Emerging Markets: Economic developments in emerging markets can present investment opportunities and risks for global investors.

10.5 Market Sentiment and Behavioral Finance:

Market sentiment refers to the overall attitude of investors towards the stock market. Positive sentiment can drive bullish trends, while negative sentiment can lead to bearish trends.

Understanding behavioral finance helps investors recognize the psychological factors influencing market sentiment, such as fear, greed, and herd mentality. Investors can use this knowledge to avoid impulsive decisions driven by emotions and adhere to their investment plans.

Conclusion:

Chapter 10 has explored market analysis and macroeconomic factors influencing the stock market. Understanding macro influences allows investors to navigate potential risks and opportunities stemming from economic trends.

By considering economic indicators, business cycles, global economic trends, and market sentiment, investors gain valuable insights into the market environment and can refine their investment strategies accordingly.

As investors progress through this book, they should continue to monitor market trends and macroeconomic developments to make informed investment decisions. Combining market analysis with a comprehensive understanding of investment strategies, risk management, and behavioral finance, investors can navigate the stock market with confidence and work towards achieving their financial goals.

Chapter 11:
Psychology in Investing - Understanding Behavioral Biases

Introduction:

Chapter 11 focuses on the critical role of psychology in investing and the impact of behavioral biases on decision-making. Investors' emotions and cognitive biases can significantly influence their investment choices, leading to irrational and suboptimal decisions. By understanding these behavioral biases and applying techniques to mitigate their effects, investors can make more rational and disciplined investment decisions.

11.1 Behavioral Finance:

The Intersection of Psychology and Investing: Behavioral finance is a field of study that explores how psychological factors and human behavior influence financial decisions. Traditional finance assumes that investors are rational and make decisions based on maximizing utility. However, behavioral finance acknowledges that investors often deviate from rationality due to emotions and cognitive biases.

Understanding behavioral finance helps investors recognize and address their biases, ultimately leading to more informed investment choices.

11.3 Emotional Investing:

Fear and Greed: Fear and greed are powerful emotions that can drive investor behavior and influence market trends. Fear of losses may cause investors to panic sell during market downturns, while greed may lead to speculative buying during market booms.

Emotional investing can result in buying at market tops and selling at market bottoms, leading to suboptimal performance. Developing emotional intelligence and managing emotions are essential for maintaining discipline and long-term investment success.

11.4 Cognitive Biases:

Cognitive biases are mental shortcuts that influence decision-making. Some common cognitive biases include:

Representativeness Bias: Making judgments based on past experiences or stereotypes rather than objective data.

Availability Bias: Relying on information that is readily available in memory, often leading to incomplete or biased decision-making.

Anchoring Bias: Placing undue importance on the first piece of information received (anchor) when making subsequent decisions.

Understanding cognitive biases helps investors critically assess information and make more rational investment choices.

11.5 Heuristics in Investing:

Heuristics are mental shortcuts that simplify decision-making. In investing, some common heuristics include:

Familiarity Bias: Preferring familiar assets or companies, even if there are better opportunities elsewhere.

Representativeness Heuristic: Assuming that a company's past performance will continue in the future.

Herding Heuristic: Following the actions of the crowd without independent analysis.

While heuristics can be useful in certain situations, they can also lead to biases and suboptimal investment decisions.

11.6 Mitigating Behavioral Biases:

To mitigate behavioral biases, investors can employ various techniques:

Educate Yourself: Understanding behavioral biases and their impact on decision-making is the first step towards mitigating them.

Stick to a Plan: Having a well-defined investment plan helps avoid impulsive decisions during market fluctuations.

Set Realistic Goals: Establishing achievable investment objectives reduces the influence of emotional factors.

Diversify Your Portfolio: A diversified portfolio can cushion the impact of individual asset fluctuations and reduce emotional responses to short-term market movements.

Avoid Emotional Triggers: Limit exposure to financial news and noise that may trigger emotional responses.

Seek Professional Advice: Working with a financial advisor can provide objective guidance and help keep emotions in check.

Summary

"Navigating the Bulls and Bears: A Guide to Stock Market Success" is a comprehensive book that equips readers with the knowledge and strategies to excel in the stock market. The book begins with an introduction to the stock market, its functions, and the significance of investing in stocks and securities.

Throughout the book, readers explore a wide range of topics, starting with stock exchanges and trading, understanding different types of stocks, and the participation of various market players. They also gain insights into market indexes, factors influencing stock prices, and the significance of market regulators in maintaining a fair market.

The book covers investment strategies suitable for beginners and seasoned investors alike, including long-term investing, value investing, growth investing, dividend investing, income investing, and index investing with exchange-traded funds (ETFs). Additionally, it delves into sector rotation and contrarian investing.

Advanced topics, such as technical analysis and fundamental analysis, are introduced to provide readers with comprehensive tools for evaluating market trends and company performance. The importance of risk management and diversification is emphasized, along with the identification and mitigation of behavioral biases in investment decision-making.

Furthermore, the book addresses macroeconomic influences on the stock market, understanding business cycles, and global economic trends that impact investments. It highlights the significance of contingency planning, regular portfolio review, and adhering to a well-defined investment plan to achieve financial goals.

Overall, "Navigating the Bulls and Bears: A Guide to Stock Market Success" serves as a comprehensive guide for investors seeking to navigate the complexities of the stock market with confidence, making informed decisions, and achieving long-term success in their investment journey.